READY TO LEARN

Kindergarten

Math

Workbook

Table of Contents

Kindergarten Math Readiness 2
Understanding Numbers Game 3
Understanding Numbers 1-5 4
Counting Numbers 1-5 14
Understanding Numbers 6-10 16
Counting Numbers 6-10 26
Understanding Numbers 11-20 28
Adding Numbers 1-10 32
Subtracting Numbers 1-10 38
Shapes 42
Understanding Measurement 46
Understanding Time 50
Sorting and Categorizing 52
Number Tracing 58
Answer Key 59
Certificate of Achievement 64

Kindergarten Math Readiness

Research shows that certain kinds of parent-child interactions in a child's early years, commonly referred to as "number talk," can be a primary driver of mathematical ability through fifth grade. Follow the directions for the games and activities throughout this book and watch your child's mathematical abilities grow!

Vocabulary Builder

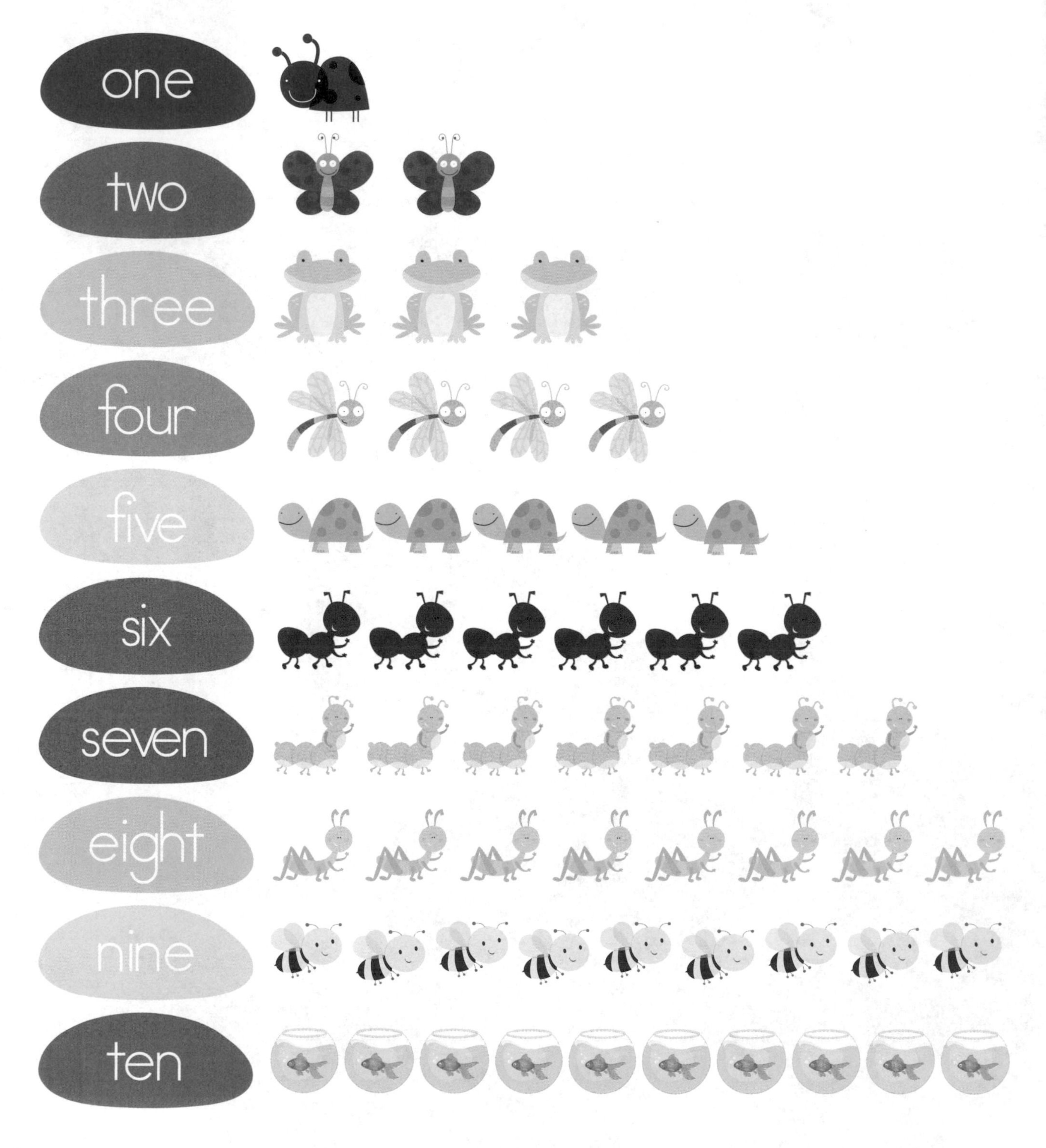

Understanding Numbers Game

Make your way from the car to the campground by following the path of numbers 1-20 in the correct order. Make sure to point to each number as you say it!

Understanding Numbers 1–5

Trace the number 1 and the word one with your finger. Then practice writing the number and the word on the lines below.

Understanding Numbers 1–5

Count the insects and write the number 1 and the word one on the lines below.

Understanding Numbers 1–5

Trace the number 2 and the word two with your finger. Then practice writing the number and the word on the lines below.

Practice writing the number 2 on the lines below.

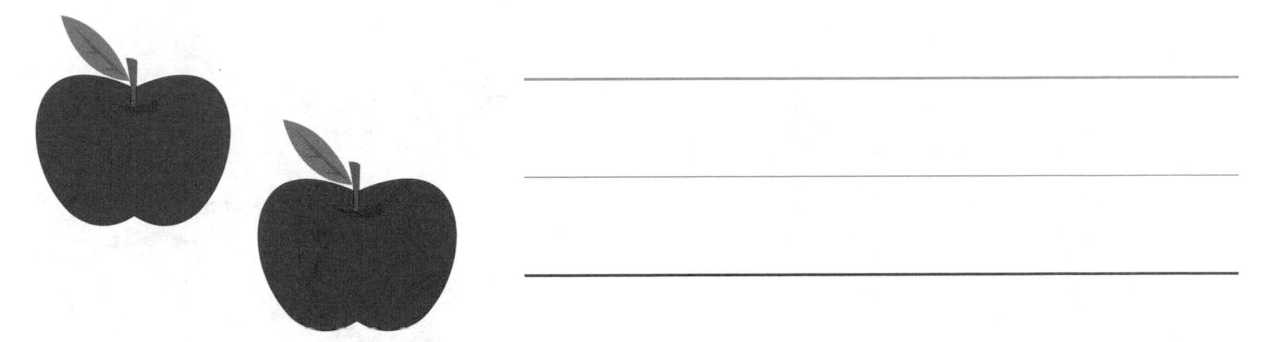

Circle the set of two apples below.

Understanding Numbers 1–5

Trace the number 3 and the word three with your finger. Then practice writing the number and the word on the lines below.

Understanding Numbers 1–5

Circle each set of three dogs. Practice writing the number 3 on the lines below.

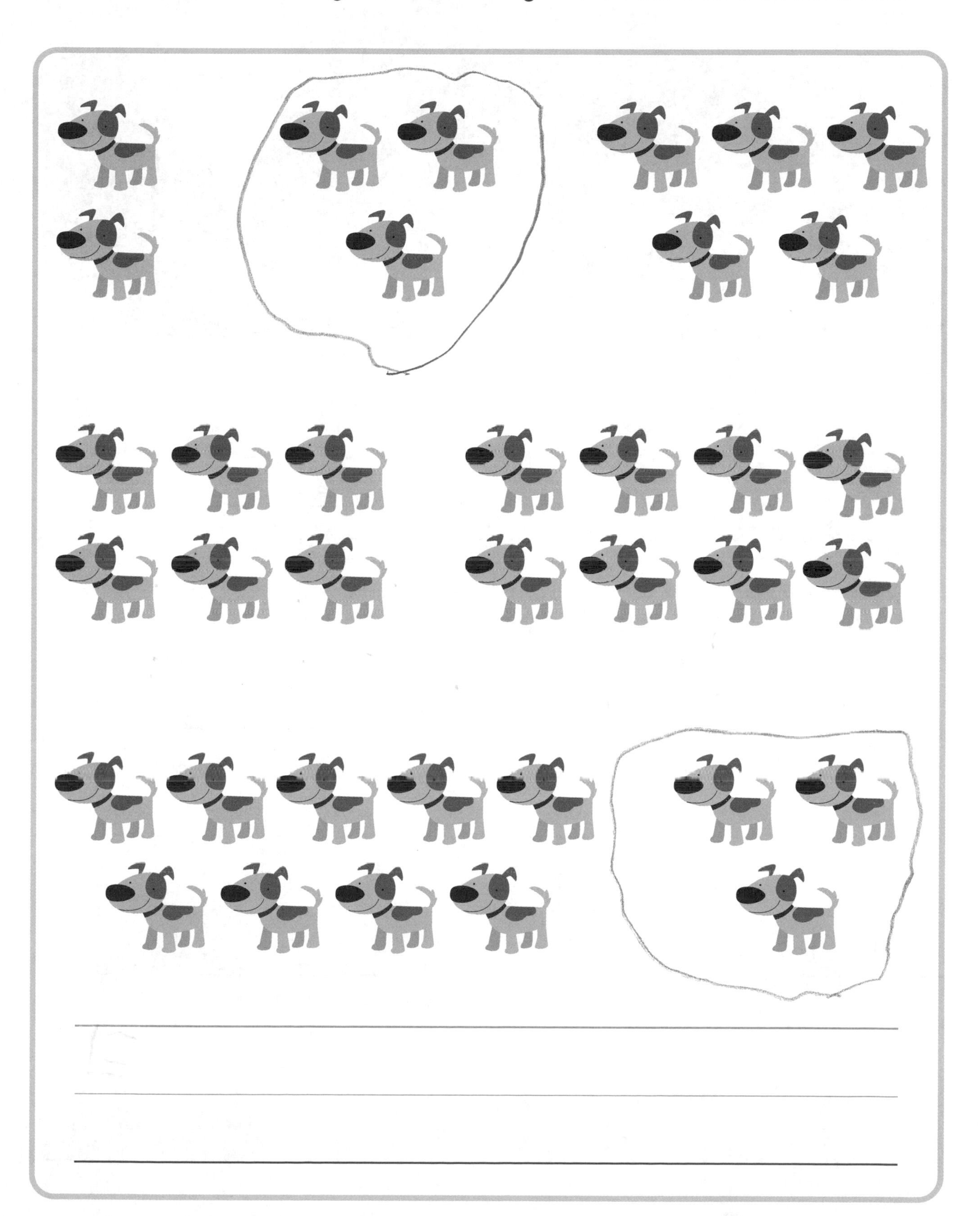

Understanding Numbers 1–5

Trace the number 4 and the word four with your finger. Then practice writing the number and the word on the lines below.

Understanding Numbers 1–5

Where are the chocolate chips? Draw four chocolate chips on the cookie. Practice writing the number 4 on the lines below.

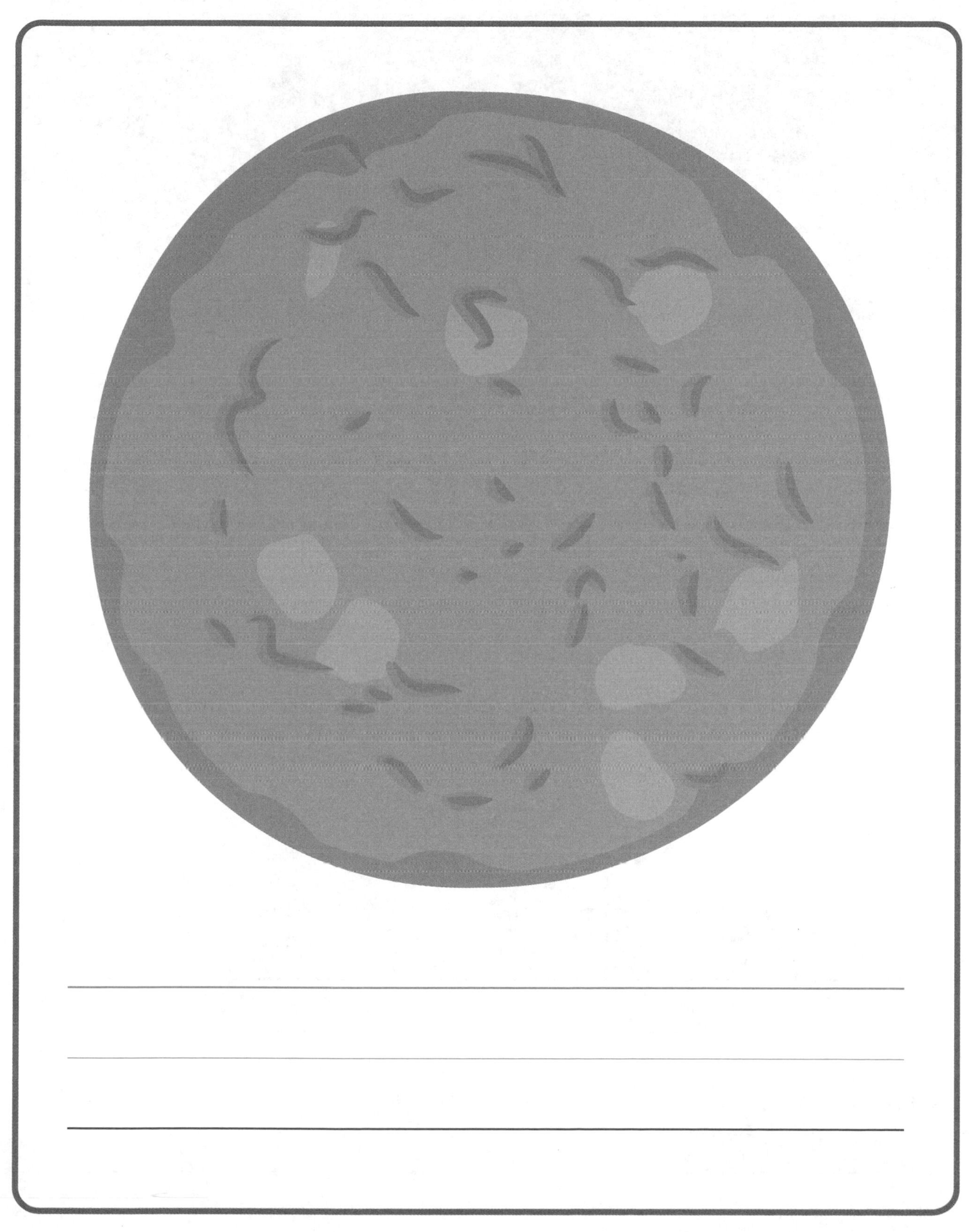

Understanding Numbers 1–5

Trace the number 5 and the word five with your finger. Then practice writing the number and the word on the lines below.

Understanding Numbers 1–5

How many swans are in the pond? Count the swans. Then color the swans and write the number on the lines below.

Counting Numbers 1–5

Count the objects and write the number and the word on the lines below.

Counting Numbers 1–5

Trace the numbers below. Then draw a line from the number to the matching set of objects.

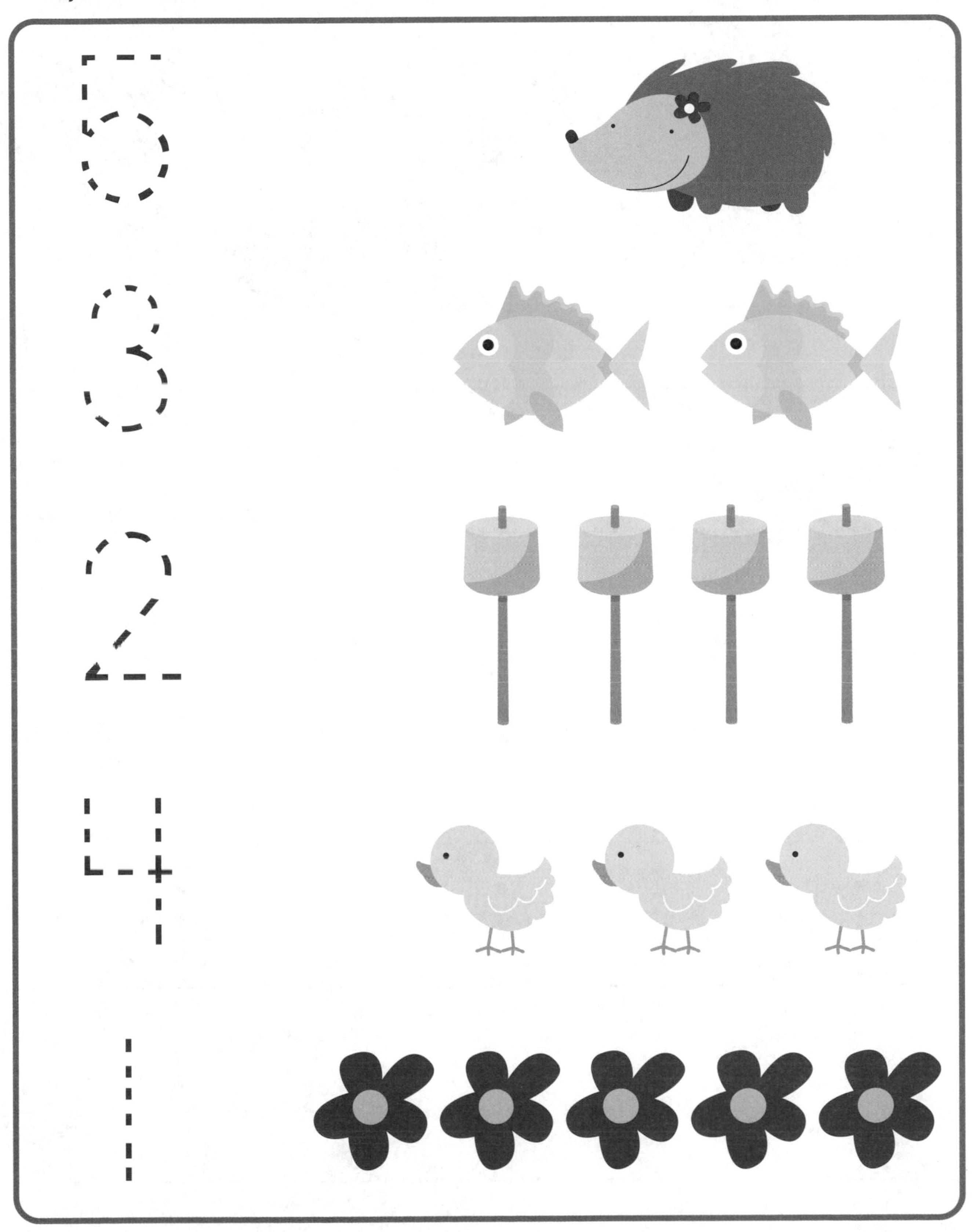

Understanding Numbers 6–10

Trace the number 6 and the word six with your finger. Then practice writing the number and the word on the lines below.

Understanding Numbers 6–10

Count the animals and write the number on the lines below.

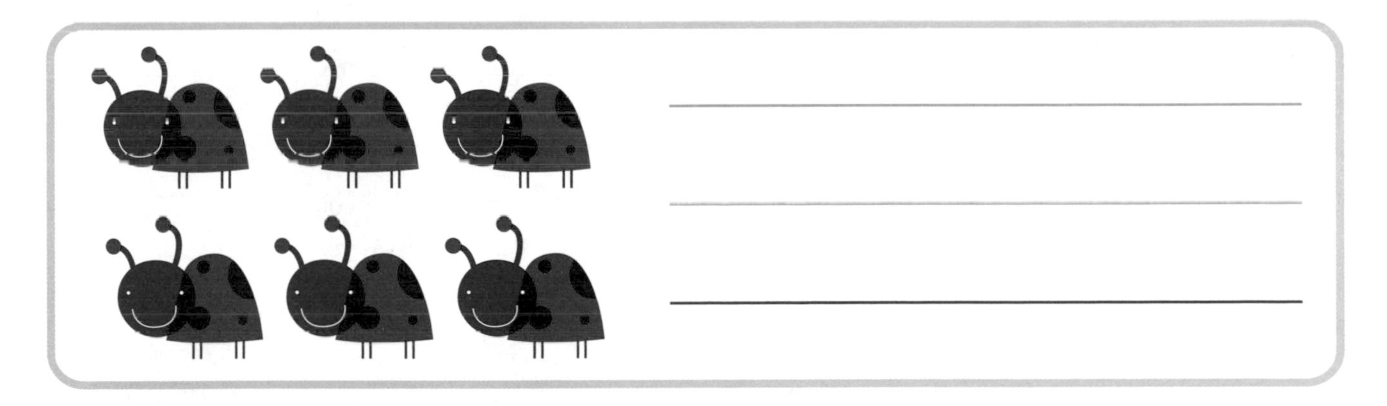

Understanding Numbers 6–10

Trace the number 7 and the word seven with your finger. Then practice writing the number and the word on the lines below.

seven seven seven

seven

Practice writing the number 7 on the lines below.

Circle each set of seven fruits below.

Understanding Numbers 6–10

Trace the number 8 and the word eight with your finger. Then practice writing the number and the word on the lines below.

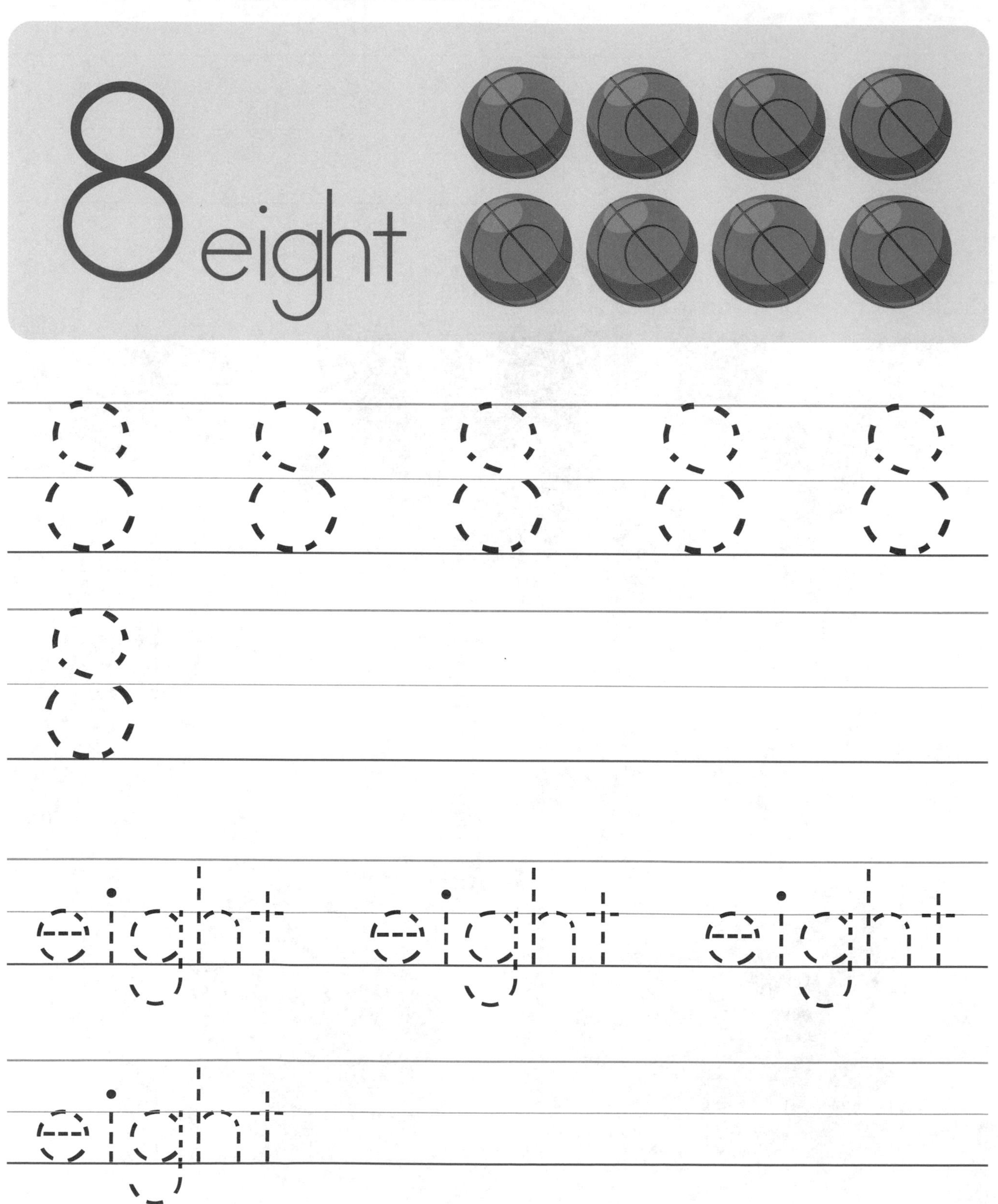

Circle each set of eight cats. Practice writing the number 8 on the lines below.

Trace the number 9 and the word nine with your finger. Then practice writing the number and word on the lines below.

Understanding Numbers 6–10

Where are the balloons? Draw nine balloons on top of the strings. Practice writing the number 9 on the lines below.

Understanding Numbers 6–10

Trace the number 10 and the word ten with your finger. Then practice writing the number and the word on the lines below.

How many leaves are on the tree? Count the leaves. Then color the leaves and write the number on the lines below.

Counting Numbers 6–10

Count the vehicles and write the number on the lines below.

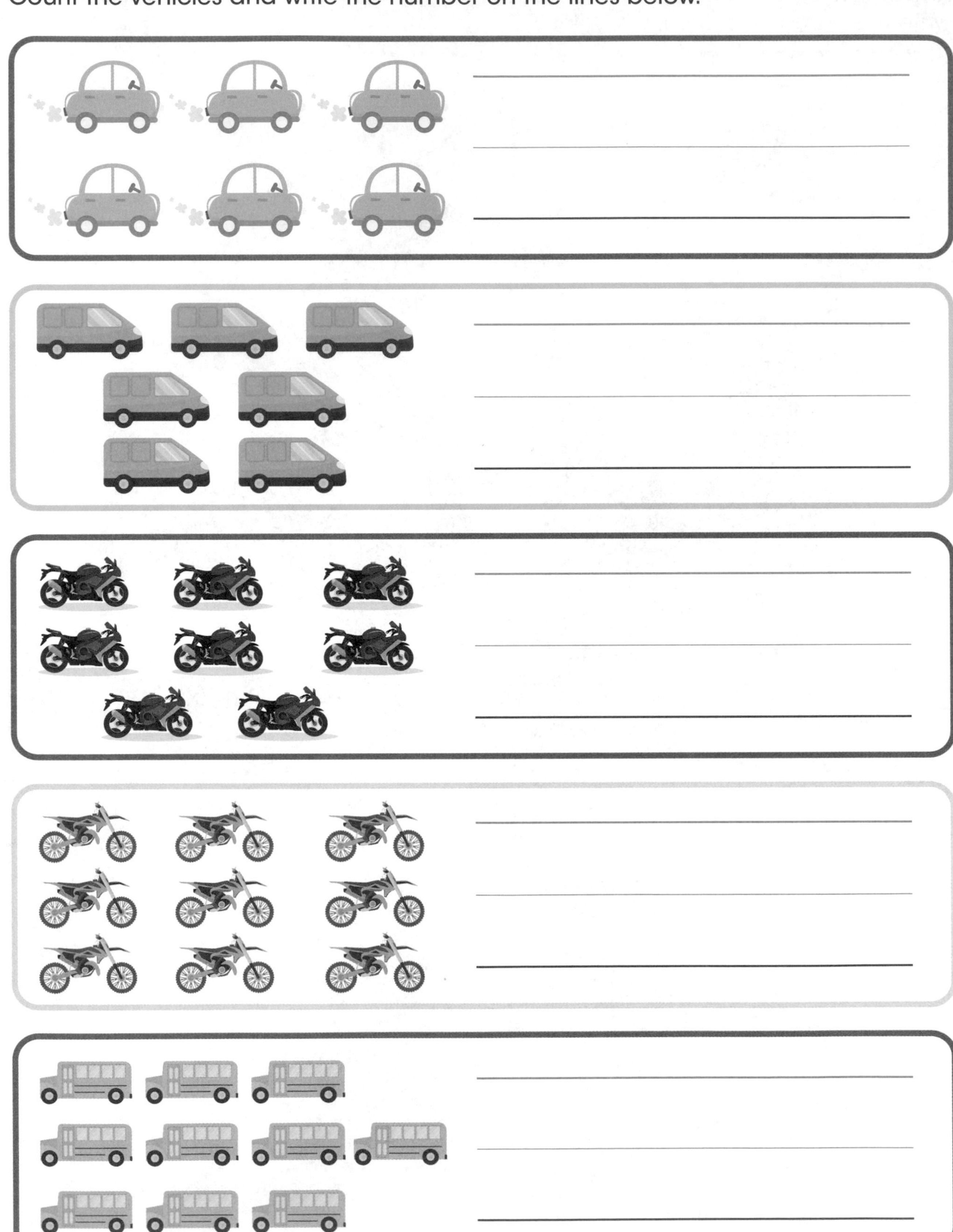

Counting Numbers 6–10

Trace the numbers below. Then draw a line from the number to the matching set of objects.

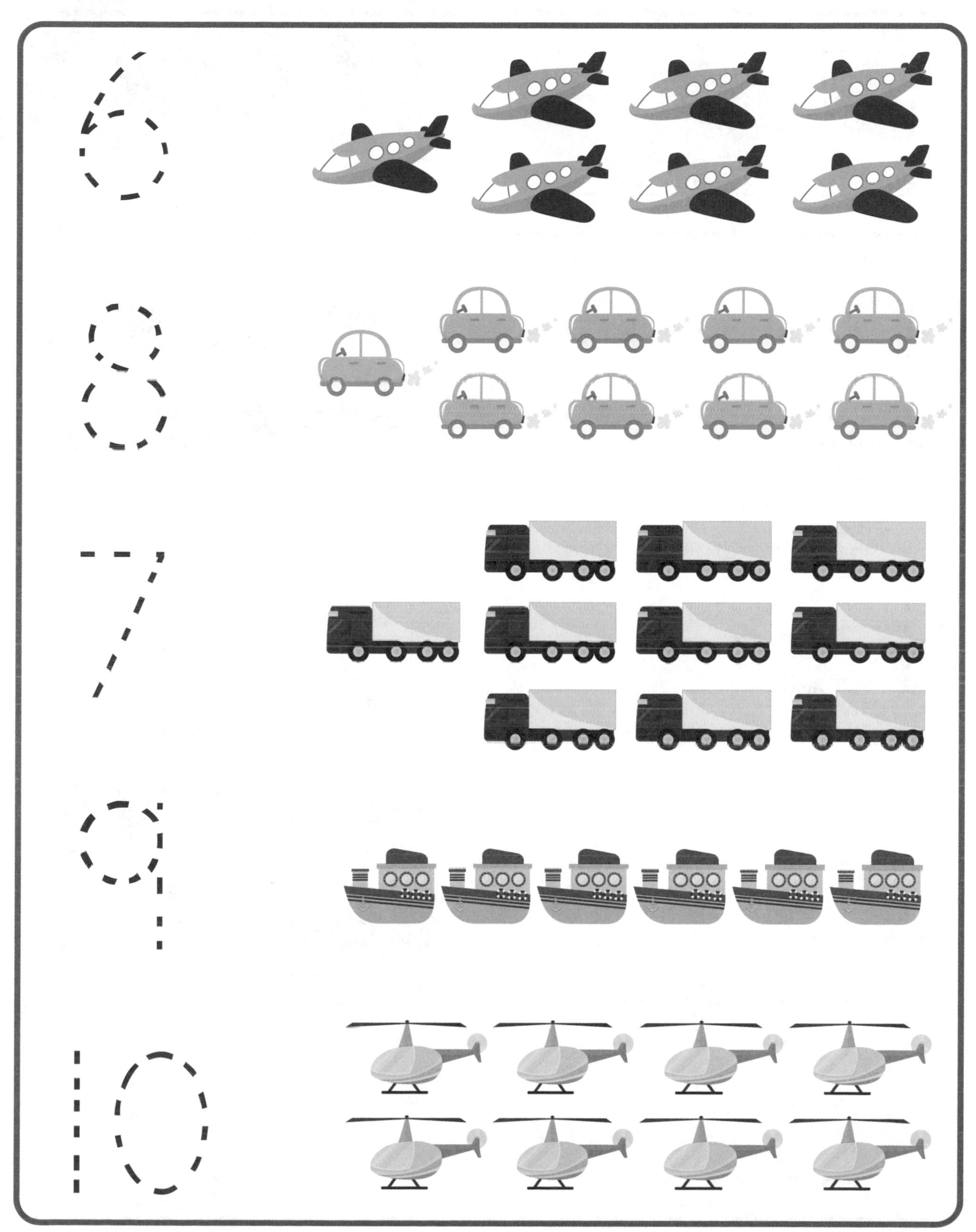

Understanding Numbers 11–20

Count the pictures. Then trace the numbers with your finger and practice writing the numbers with a pencil on the lines below.

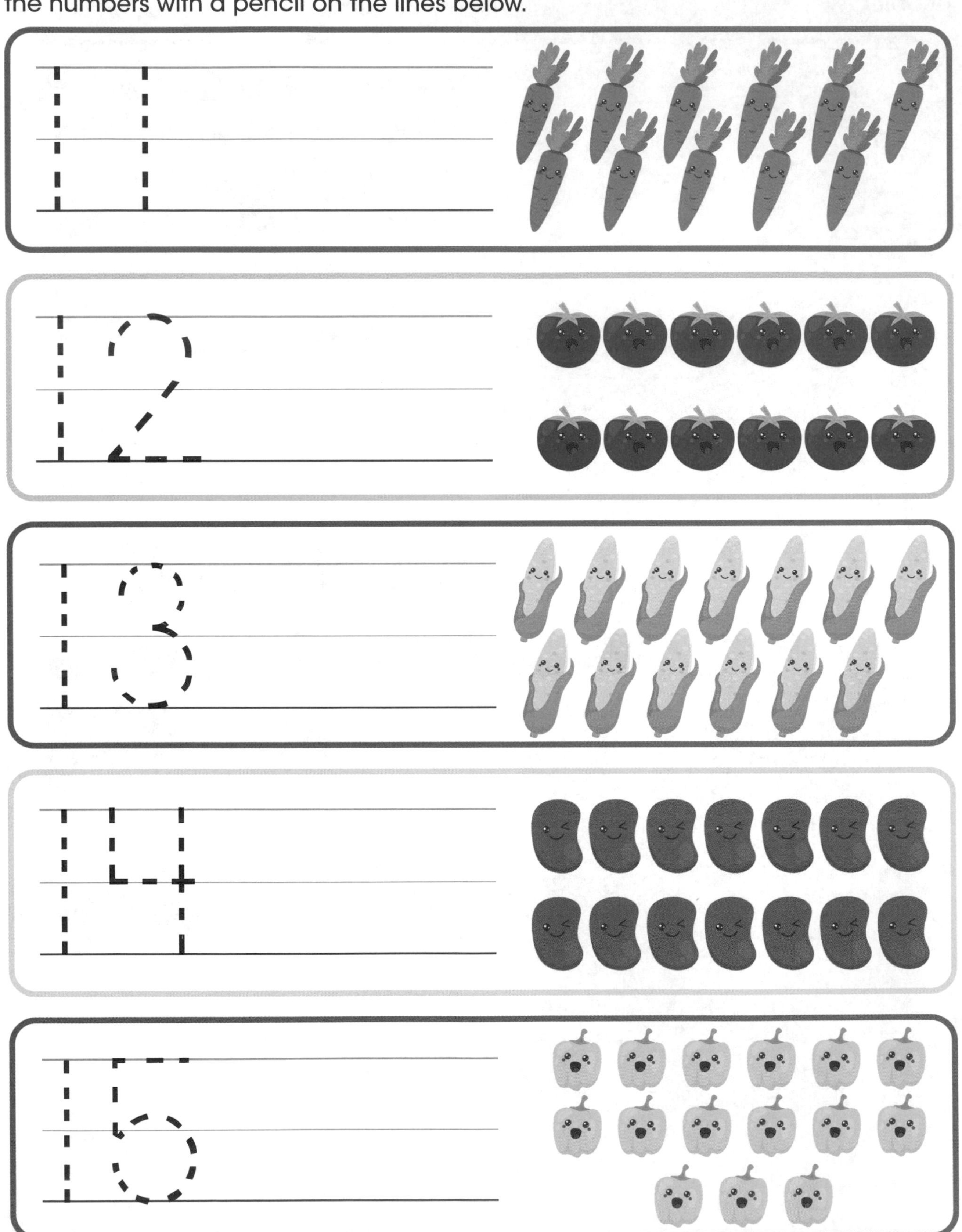

Understanding Numbers 11–20

Count the objects and circle the correct number below each set of pictures.

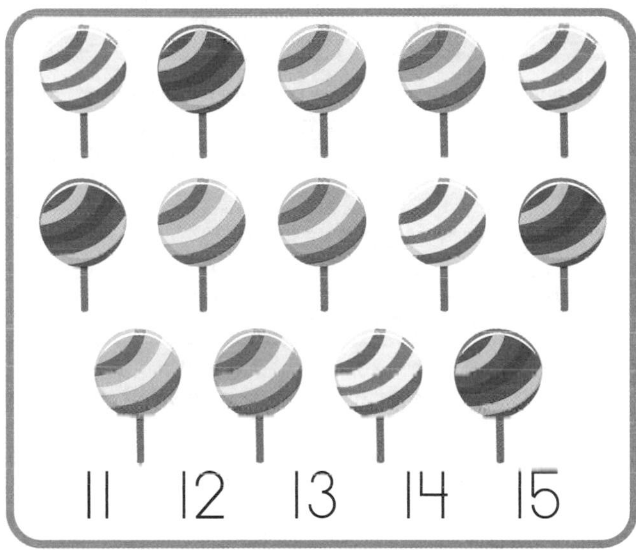

Understanding Numbers 11–20

Count the pictures. Then trace the numbers with your finger and practice writing the numbers with a pencil on the lines below.

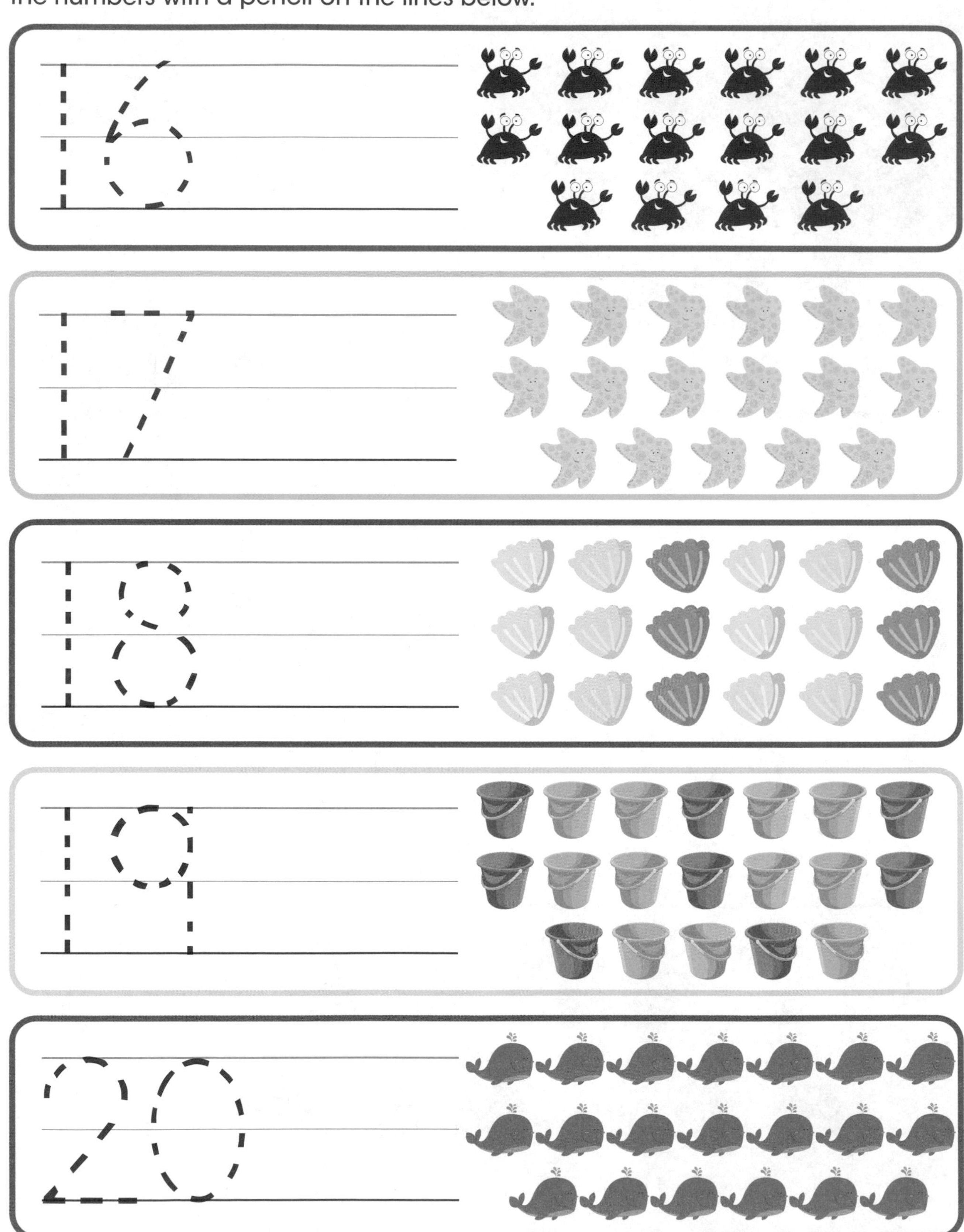

Understanding Numbers 11–20

Count the objects and circle the correct number below each set of pictures.

16 17 18 19 20

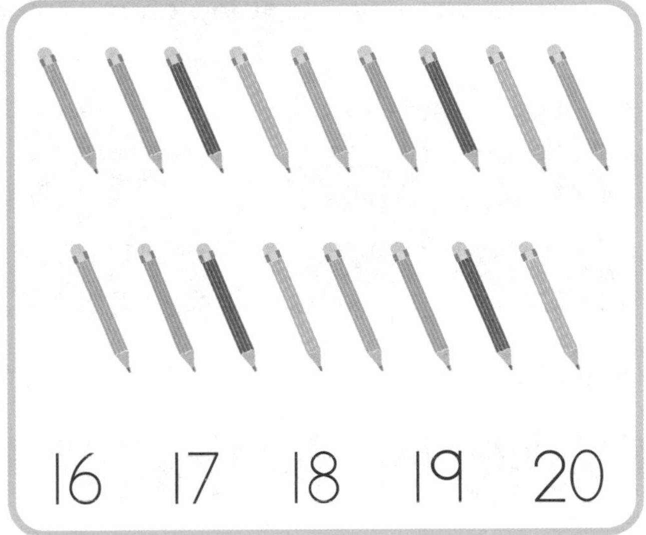

16 17 18 19 20

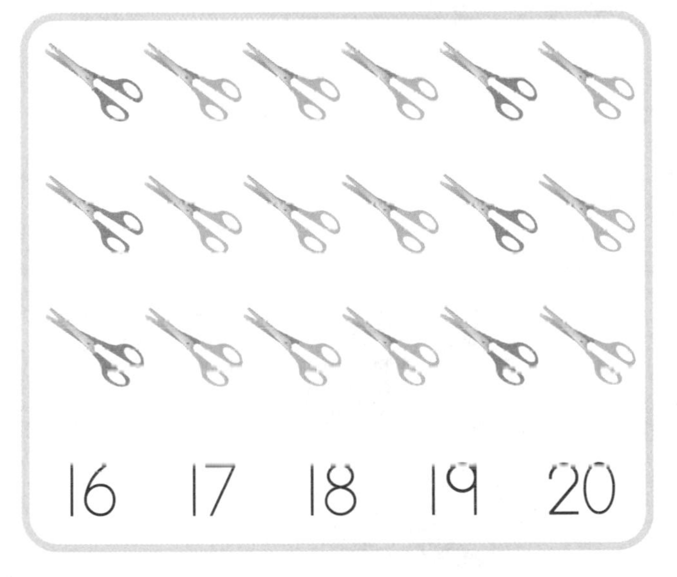

16 17 18 19 20

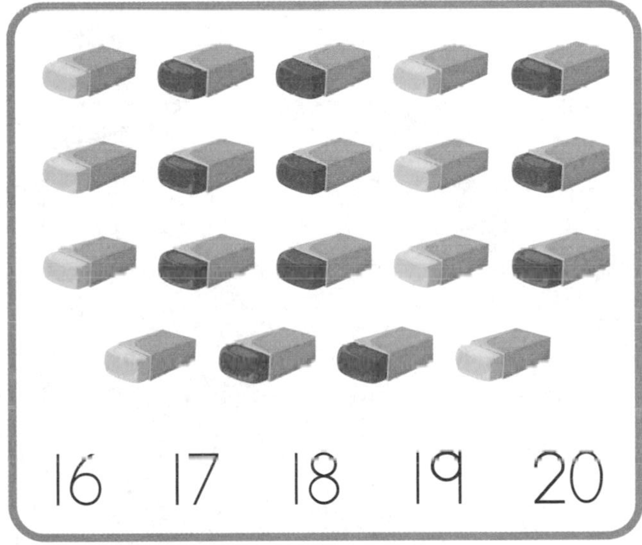

16 17 18 19 20

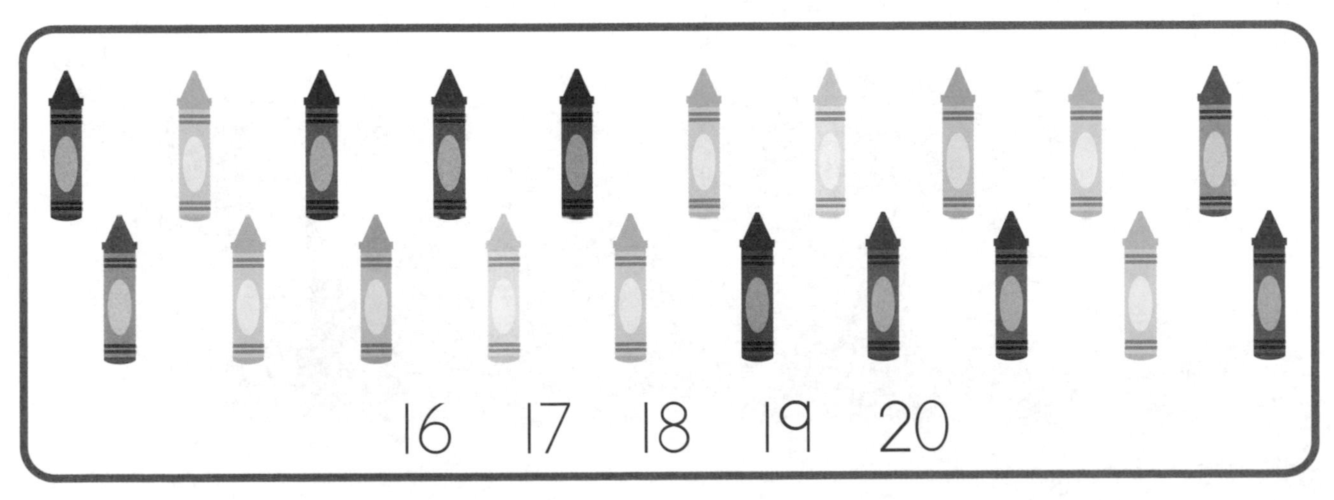

16 17 18 19 20

Adding Numbers 1–10

Adding and subtracting are skills that your child can learn using pictures or real objects. Singing songs is another great way to learn these skills! Try singing "Five Little Monkeys Jumping on a Bed" to practice!

Vocabulary Builder

add	putting two numbers together
in all	the total amount of the numbers put together
subtract	taking away a number from an amount
are left	the amount you have after taking a number away

Adding Numbers 1–10

Point to and count the kids who are swinging. Write the number on the lines below. Count how many kids are jumping rope and write the number on the lines below. How many kids are playing in all? Write the number on the lines below.

Adding Numbers 1–10

Point to and count the red dots. Write the number on the lines below. Count the blue dots and write the number on the lines below. How many red and blue dots are there in all? Write the number on the lines below.

How many red dots are there?

How many blue dots are there?

How many red and blue dots are there in all?

Adding Numbers 1–10

Point to and count the seashells on the beach. Write the number on the lines below. Count how many sandcastles there are and write the number on the lines below. How many seashells and sandcastles are there in all? Write the number on the lines below.

How many seashells are there?

How many sandcastles are there?

How many seashells and sandcastles are there in all?

Adding Numbers 1–10

Point to and count the green blocks you see. Write the number on the lines below. Count how many yellow blocks there are and write the number on the lines below. How many green and yellow blocks are there in all? Write the number on the lines below.

How many green blocks are there?

How many yellow blocks are there?

How many green and yellow blocks are there in all?

Adding Numbers 1–10

Point to and count the frogs you can see. Write the number on the lines below. Count how many lily pads there are and write the number on the lines below. How many frogs and lily pads are there in all? Write the number on the lines below.

How many frogs are there?

How many lily pads are there?

How many frogs and lily pads are there in all?

Subtracting Numbers 1–10

Point to and count all of the cats in the picture. Write the number on the lines below. Cross out the gray cats. How many gray cats did you cross out? How many cats are left? Write the numbers on the lines below.

How many cats are there in all?

How many gray cats did you cross out?

How many cats are left?

Subtracting Numbers 1–10

Point to and count all of the cubes below. Write the number on the lines below. Cross out the blue cubes. How many blue cubes did you cross out? How many cubes are left? Write the numbers on the lines below.

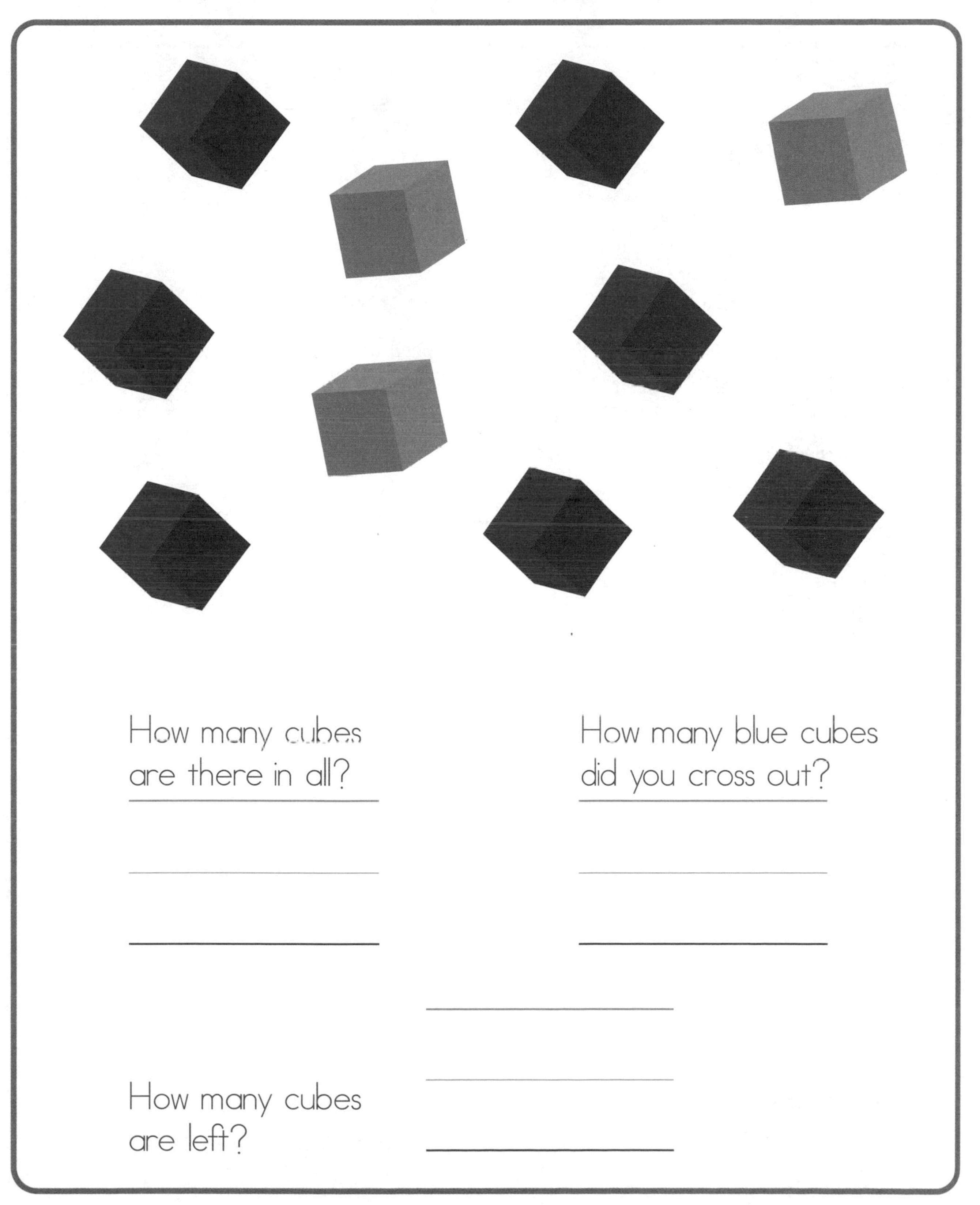

Subtracting Numbers 1–10

Point to and count all of the deer in the picture. Write the number on the lines below. Cross out the deer without spots. How many deer without spots did you cross out? How many deer are left? Write the numbers on the lines below.

How many deer are there in all?

How many deer without spots did you cross out?

How many deer are left?

Subtracting Numbers 1–10

Point to and count all of the circles. Write the number on the lines below. Cross out the yellow circles. How many yellow circles did you cross out? How many circles are left? Write the numbers on the lines below.

Shapes

Knowing the primary shapes is the foundation for building knowledge of two-dimensional and three-dimensional geometric figures. Help your child by tracing, drawing, and naming the shapes together.

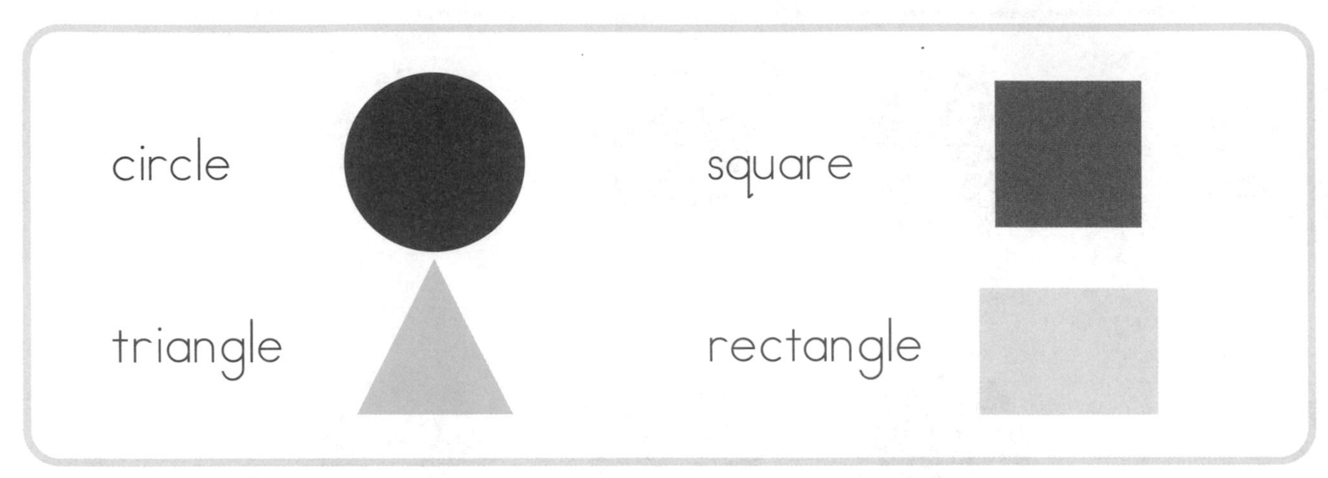

Point to and name the shapes you see in the picture below.

Name That Shape!

Circle the correct name of the shapes below.

Shapes

Count the shapes in the picture. Write the number of each shape on the lines below. Then color the shapes.

______ circles

______ squares

______ rectangles

______ triangle

Shape Jumble!

Color Key

Circle:	Red	Square:	Green
Rectangle:	Blue	Triangle:	Orange

Color the shapes below using the color key.

Understanding Measurement

We measure things in many ways every day. Conversations about how long it is until lunchtime, how far it is to the park, and how tall your child is getting will engage your child in the process of learning these skills. Before you know it, they will be telling time, measuring, and comparing sizes of objects!

Longer and Shorter

Circle the objects that are longer. Cross out the objects that are shorter.

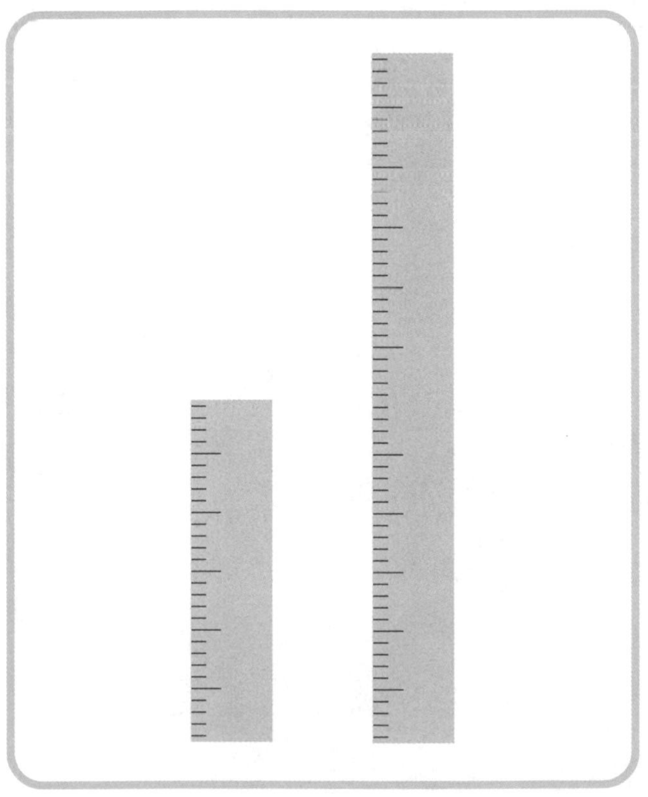

Bigger and Smaller

Circle the objects that are bigger. Cross out the objects that are smaller.

Heavier and Lighter

Circle the objects that are heavier. Cross out the objects that are lighter.

Understanding Time

What time is it? Some things happen during the day and some things happen at night. Draw a line from the time of day to the matching picture.

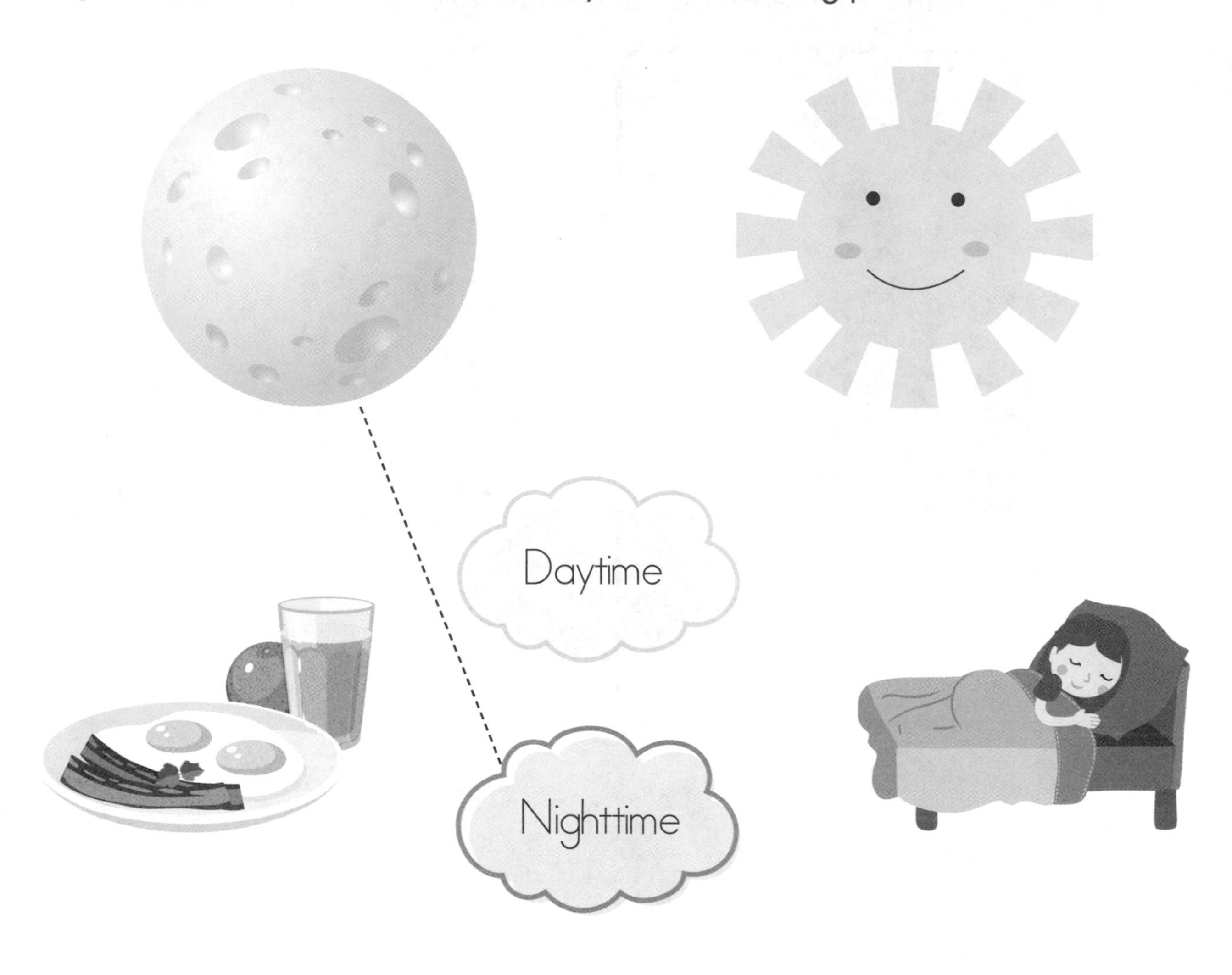

Understanding Time

Let's Talk About a Clock!

A clock has numbers from 1 to 12 on its face. Complete the picture of the clock by writing the missing numbers in the circles.

Sorting and Categorizing

Naturally, when children explore everything around them, they notice how things are alike and how things are different. Sorting and categorizing are best learned when they are part of a child's everyday life. Common activities that children experience during play and daily tasks they perform provide many opportunities for them to learn these math concepts.

Same

Circle the objects that are the same in each row.

Different

Cross out the objects that are different in each row.

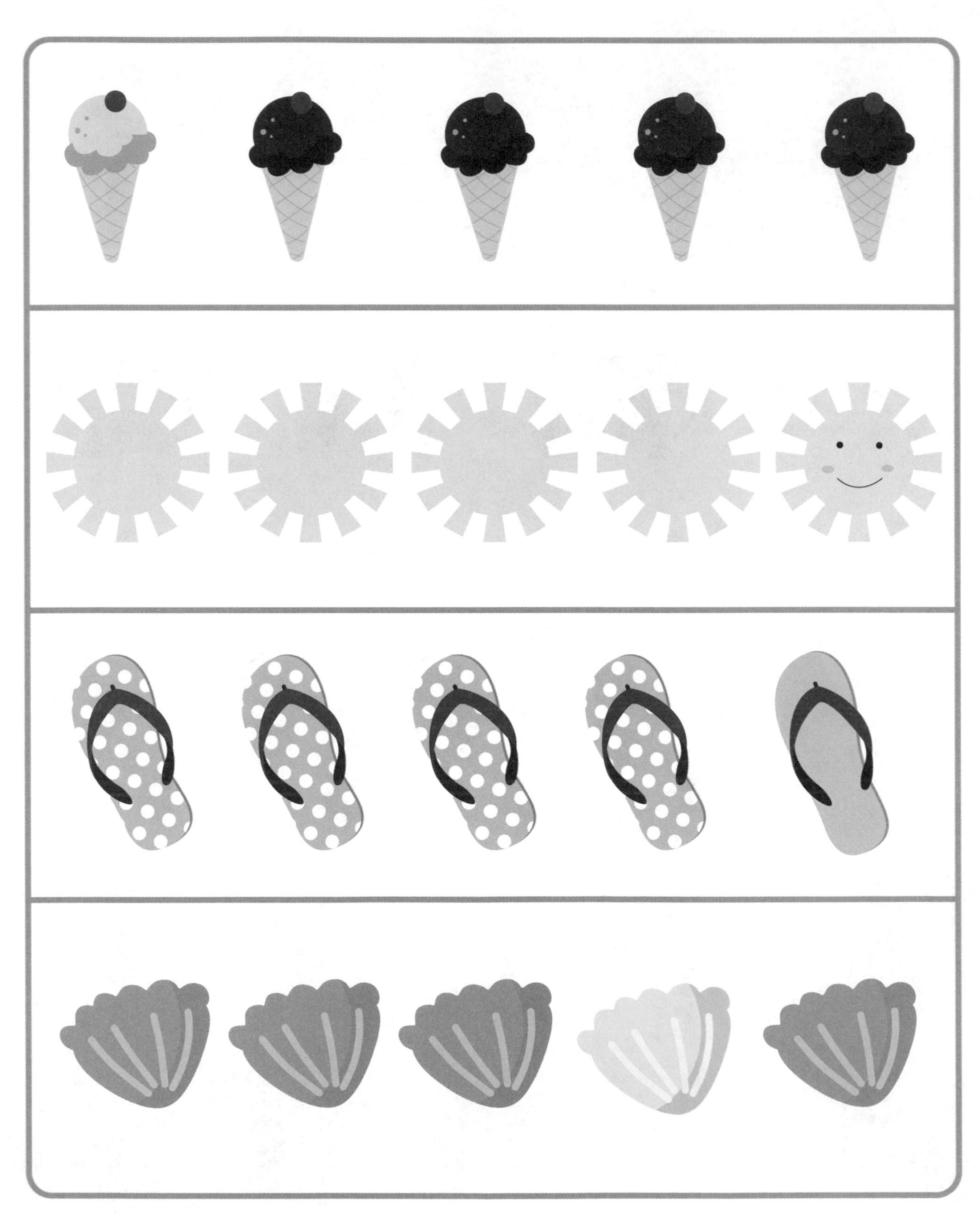

Sorting and Categorizing

One of the things in each row doesn't belong there.
Cross out the objects that don't belong.

Graphing Shapes

Color in the graph to show how many of each shape is in the picture below.

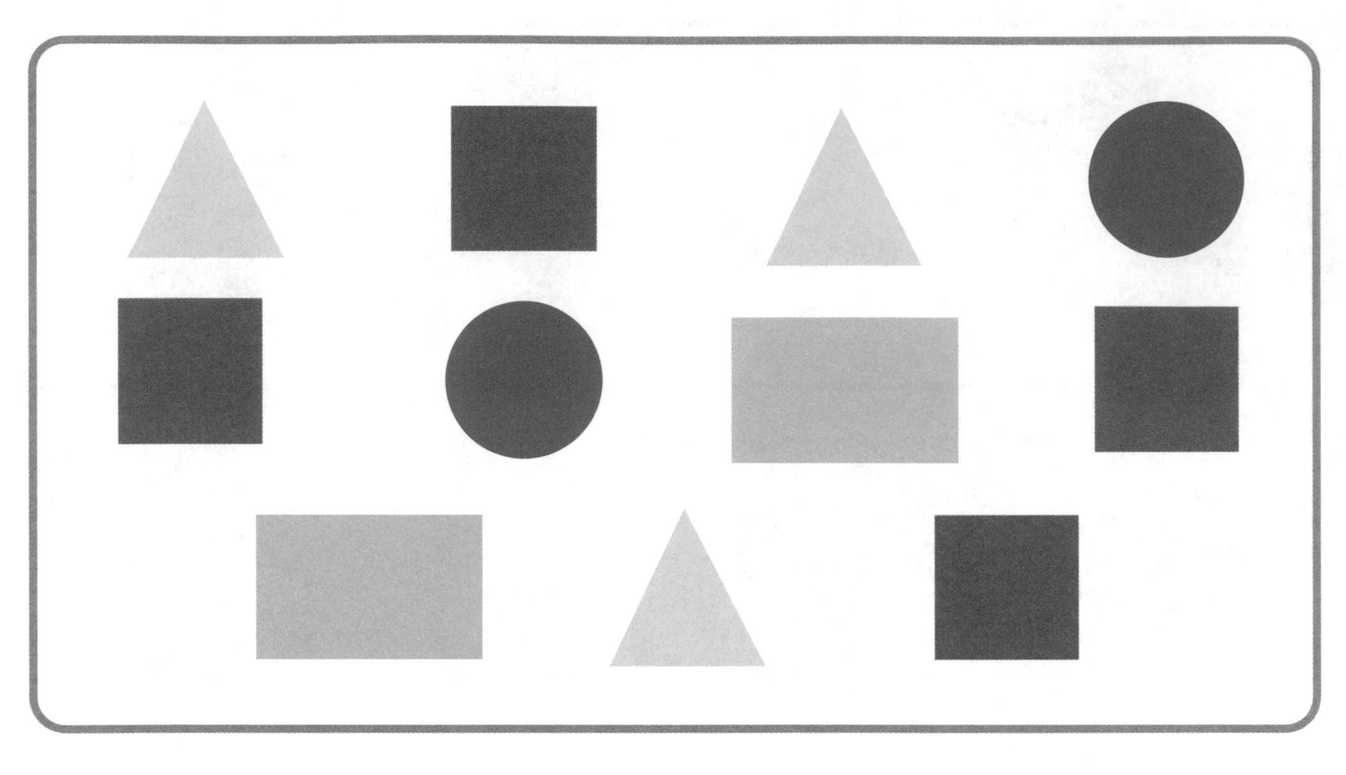

Shapes

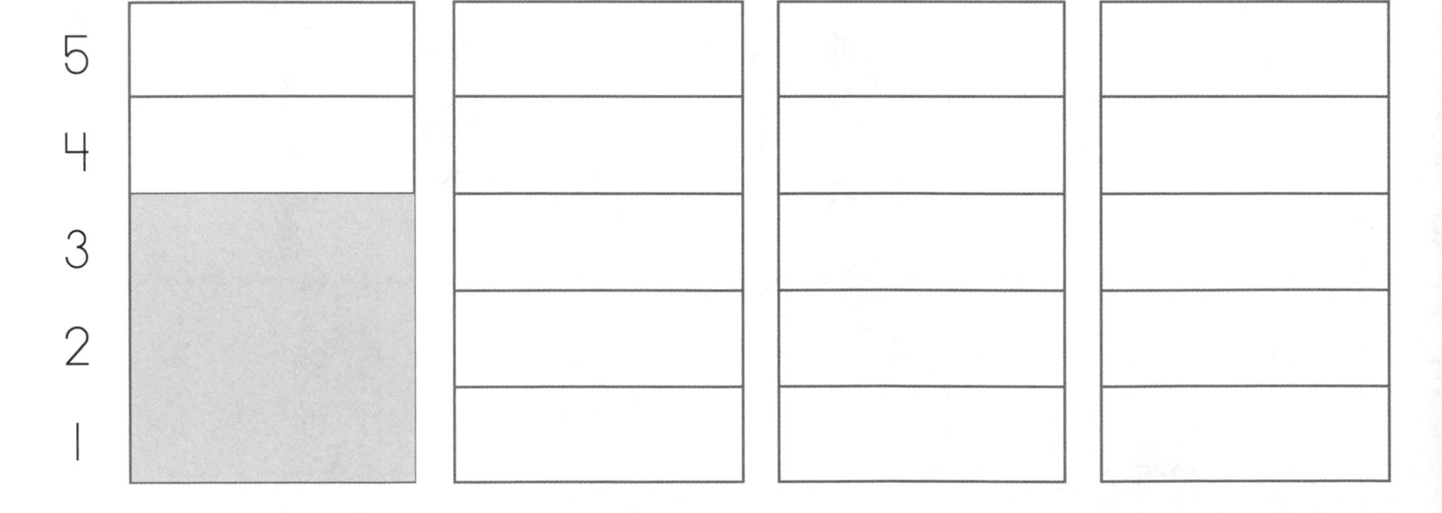

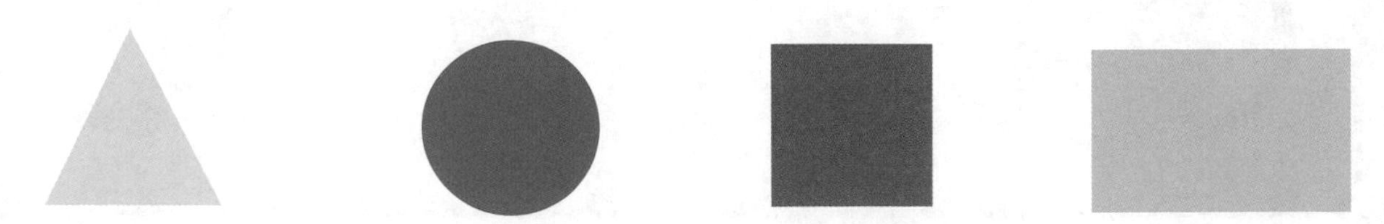

Reading a Bar Graph

Each colored section represents one person who likes that sport. Count how many votes each sport received and answer the questions below.

How many people like football? ______________________

How many people like soccer? ______________________

How many people like basketball? ______________________

How many people like baseball? ______________________

Our Favorite Sports

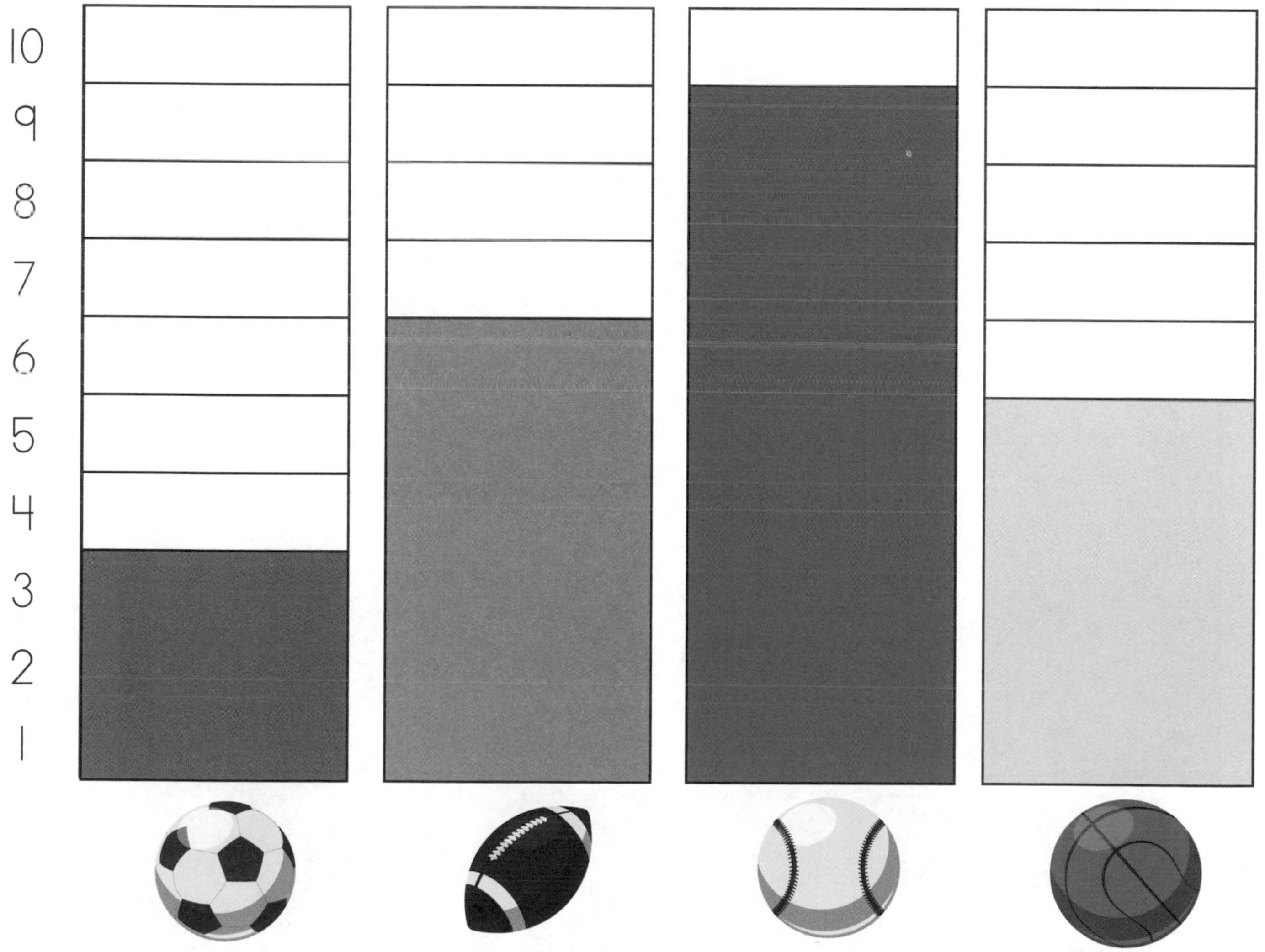

10
9
8
7
6
5
4
3
2
1

Number Tracing

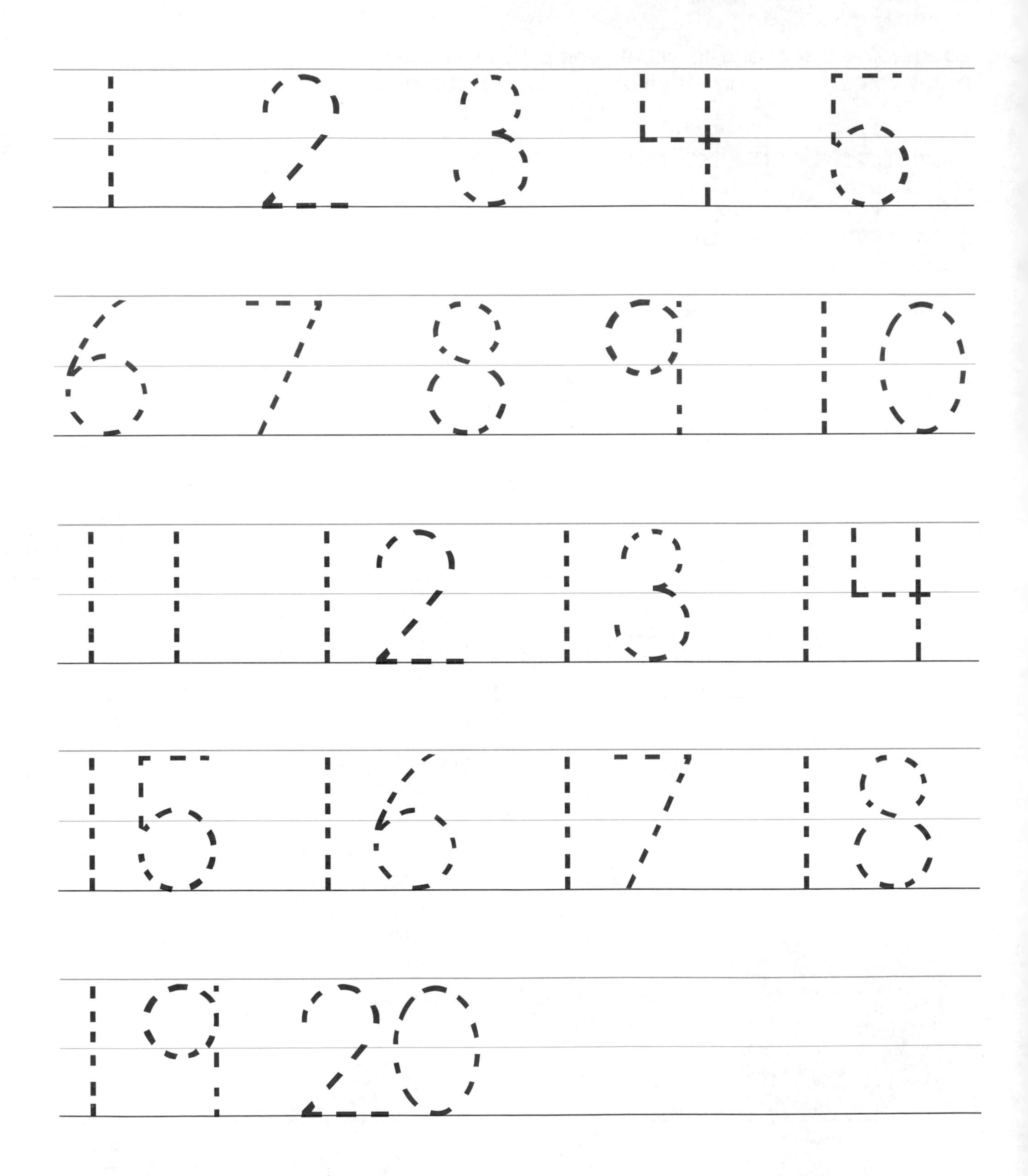

ANSWER KEY

Page 3

Understanding Numbers Game

Make your way from the car to the campground by following the path of numbers 1-20 in the correct order. Make sure to point to each number as you say it!

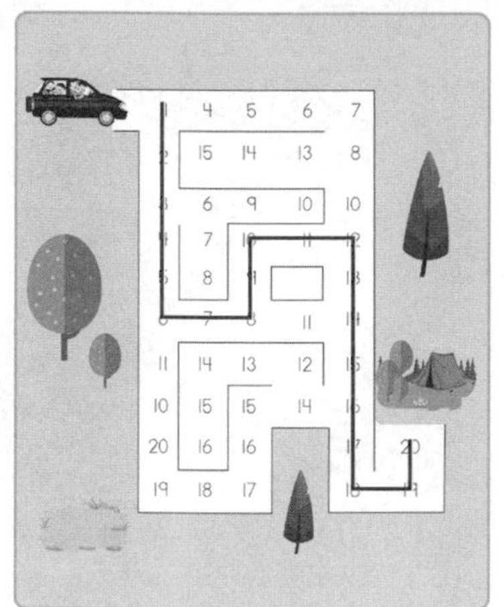

3

Page 5

Understanding Numbers 1–5

Count the insects and write the number 1 and the word one the lines below.

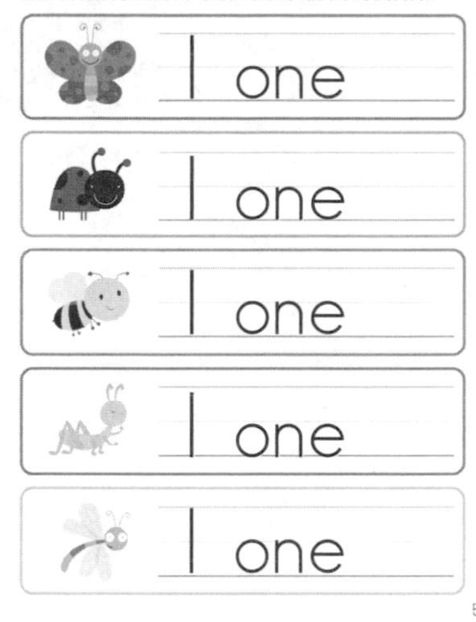

5

Page 7

Understanding Numbers 1–5

Practice writing the number 2 on the lines below.

Circle the set of two apples below.

7

Page 9

Understanding Numbers 1–5

Circle each set of three dogs. Practice writing the number 3 on the lines below.

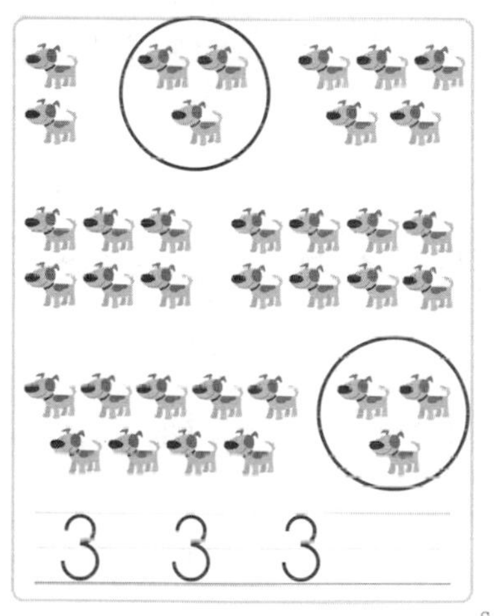

9

Page 11

Understanding Numbers 1–5

Where are the chocolate chips? Draw four chocolate chips on the cookie. Practice writing the number 4 on the lines below.

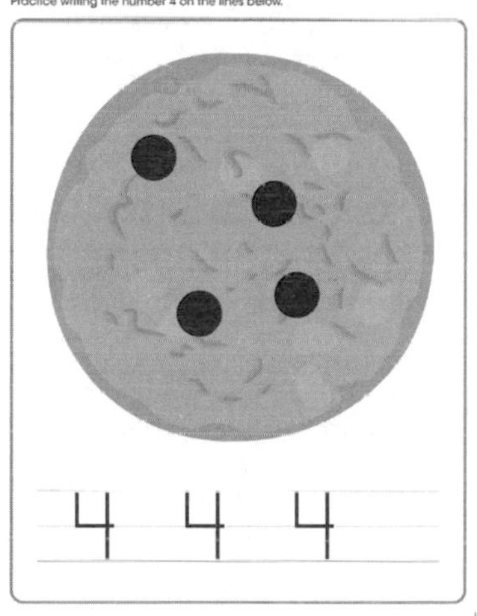

11

Page 13

Understanding Numbers 1–5

How many swans are in the pond? Count the swans. Then color the swans and write the number on the lines below.

13

Page 14

Counting Numbers 1–5

Count the objects and write the number and the word on the lines below.

14

Page 15

Counting Numbers 1–5

Trace the numbers below. Then draw a line from the number to the matching set of objects.

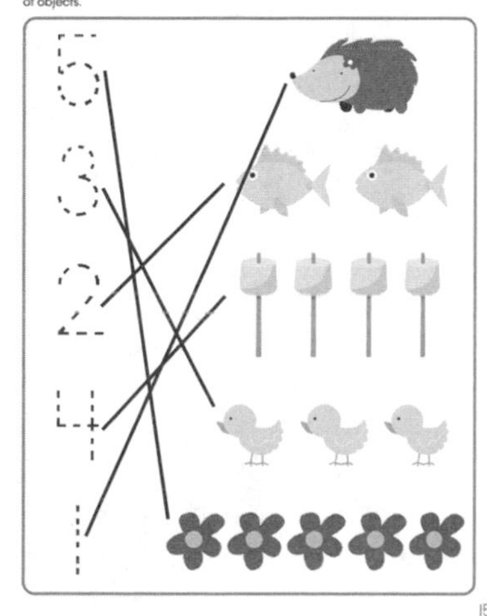

15

Page 17

Understanding Numbers 6–10

Count the animals and write the number on the lines below.

17

Page 19

Understanding Numbers 6–10

Practice writing the number 7 on the lines below.

Circle each set of seven fruits below.

19

Page 21

Understanding Numbers 6–10

Circle each set of eight cats. Practice writing the number 8 on the lines below.

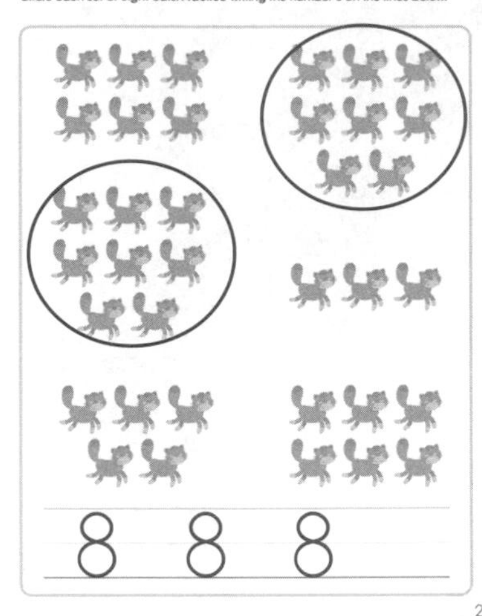

21

Page 23

Understanding Numbers 6–10

Where are the balloons? Draw nine balloons on top of the strings. Practice writing the number 9 on the lines below.

23

Page 25

Understanding Numbers 6–10

How many leaves are on the tree? Count the leaves. Then color the leaves and write the number on the lines below.

25

Page 26

Counting Numbers 6–10

Count the vehicles and write the number on the lines below.

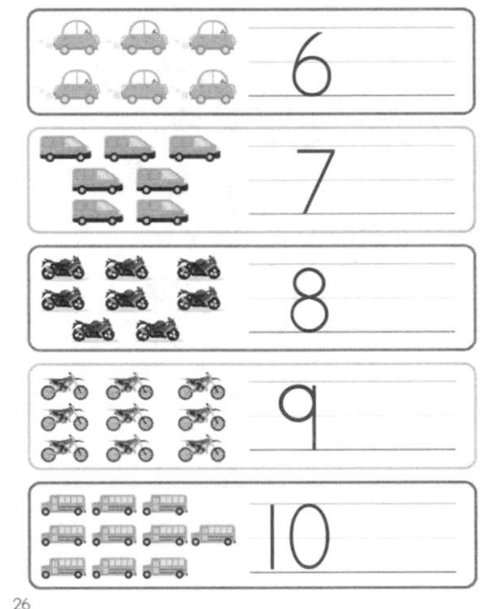

26

Page 27

Counting Numbers 6–10

Trace the numbers below. Then draw a line from the number to the matching set of objects.

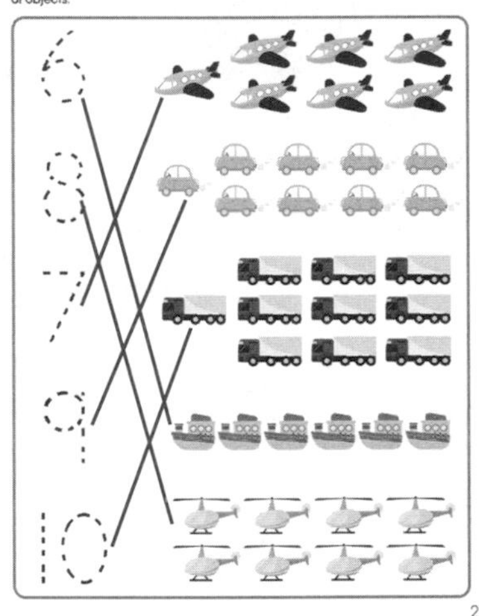

27

Page 29

Understanding Numbers 11–20

Count the objects and circle the correct number below each set of pictures.

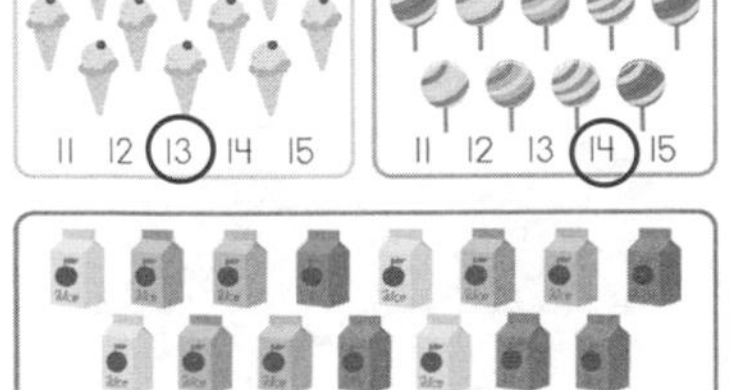

29

Page 31

Understanding Numbers 11–20

Count the objects and circle the correct number below each set of pictures.

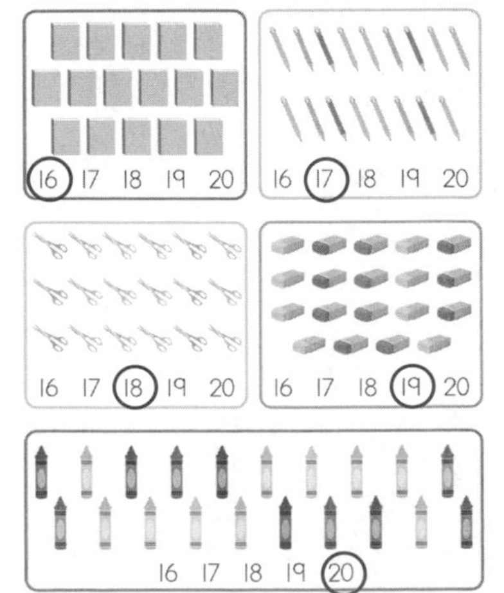

31

Page 34

Adding Numbers 1–10

Point to and count the red dots. Write the number on the lines below. Count the blue dots and write the number on the lines below. How many red and blue dots are there in all? Write the number on the lines below.

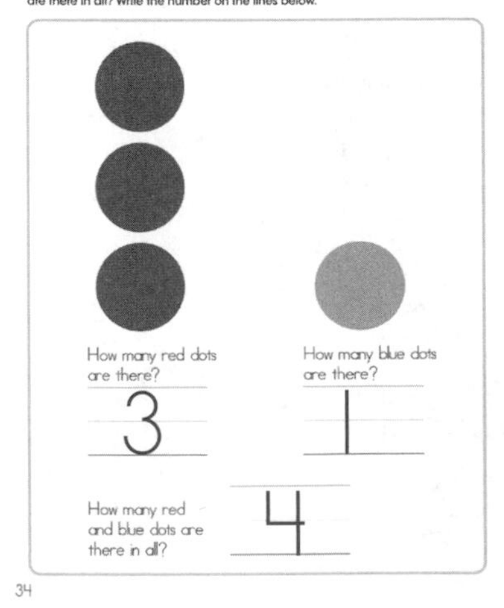

34

Page 35

Adding Numbers 1–10

Point to and count the seashells on the beach. Write the number on the lines below. Count how many sandcastles there are and write the number on the lines below. How many seashells and sandcastles are there in all? Write the number on the lines below.

Page 36

Adding Numbers 1–10

Point to and count the green blocks you see. Write the number on the lines below. Count how many yellow blocks there are and write the number on the lines below. How many green and yellow blocks are there in all? Write the number on the lines below.

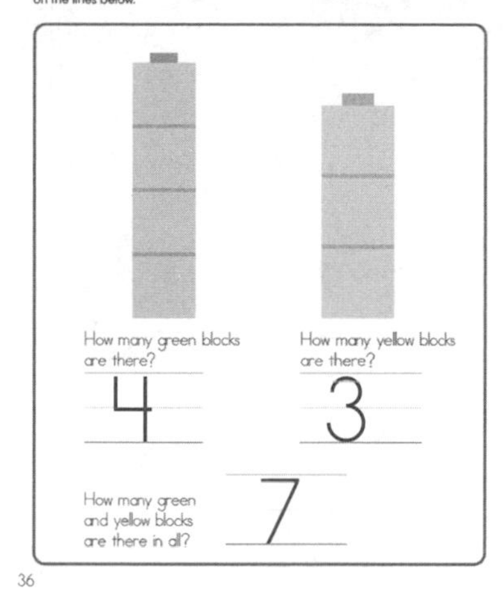

Page 37

Adding Numbers 1–10

Point to and count the frogs you can see. Write the number on the lines below. Count how many lily pads there are and write the number on the lines below. How many frogs and lily pads are there in all? Write the number on the lines below.

Page 38

Subtracting Numbers 1–10

Point to and count all of the cats in the picture. Write the number on the lines below. Cross out the gray cats. How many gray cats did you cross out? How many cats are left? Write the numbers on the lines below.

Page 39

Subtracting Numbers 1–10

Point to and count all of the cubes below. Write the number on the lines below. Cross out the blue cubes. How many blue cubes did you cross out? How many cubes are left? Write the numbers on the lines below.

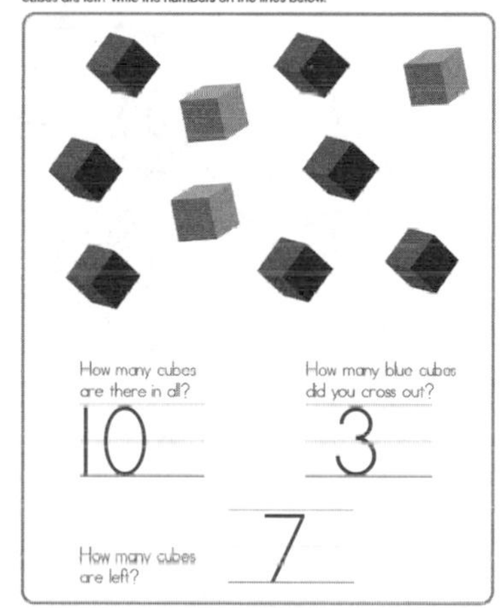

Page 40

Subtracting Numbers 1–10

Point to and count all of the deer in the picture. Write the number on the lines below. Cross out the deer without spots. How many deer without spots did you cross out? How many deer are left? Write the numbers on the lines below.

Page 41

Subtracting Numbers 1–10

Point to and count all of the circles. Write the number on the lines below. Cross out the yellow circles. How many yellow circles did you cross out? How many circles are left? Write the numbers on the lines below.

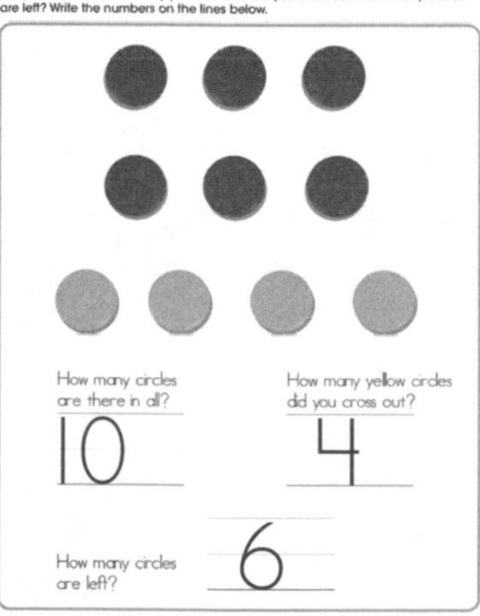

Page 43

Shapes

Name That Shape!

Circle the correct name of the shapes below.

Page 44

Shapes

Count the shapes in the picture. Write the number of each shape on the lines below. Then color the shapes.

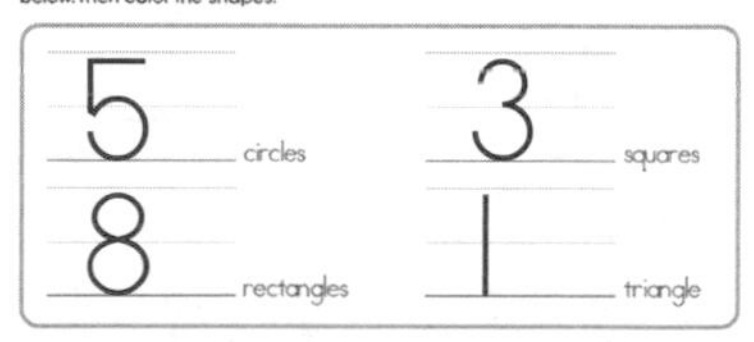

Page 45

Shapes

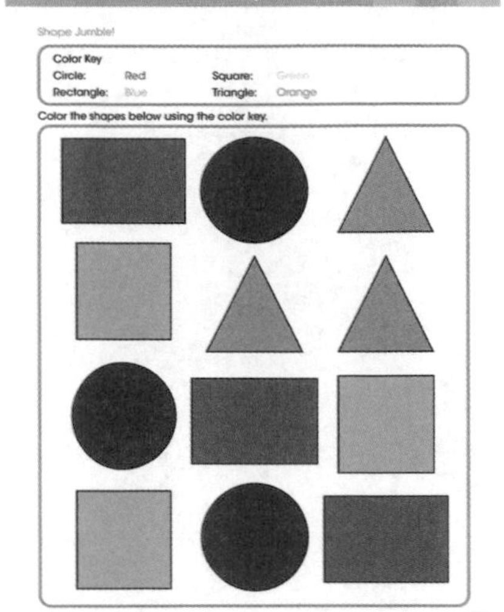

Shape Jumble!

Color Key
Circle: Red Square: Green
Rectangle: Blue Triangle: Orange

Color the shapes below using the color key.

45

Page 47

Understanding Measurement

Longer and Shorter
Circle the objects that are longer. Cross out the objects that are shorter.

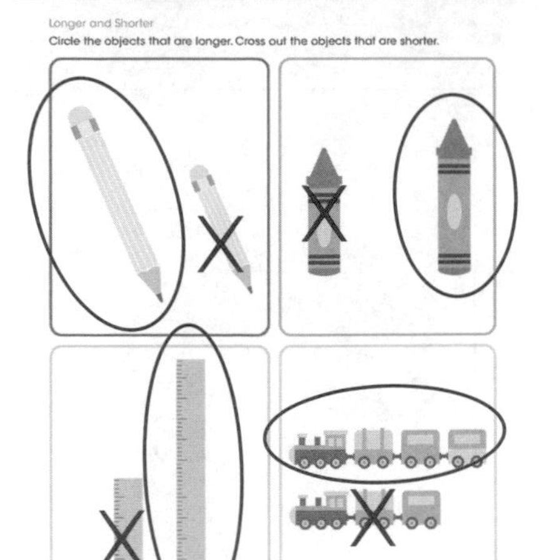

47

Page 48

Understanding Measurement

Bigger and Smaller
Circle the objects that are bigger. Cross out the objects that are smaller.

48

Page 49

Understanding Measurement

Heavier and Lighter
Circle the objects that are heavier. Cross out the objects that are lighter.

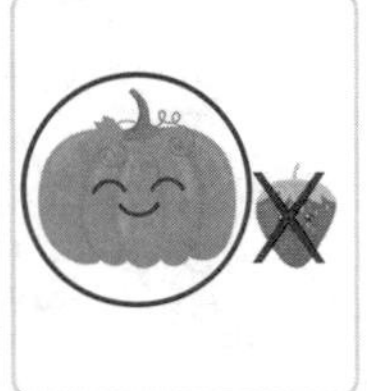

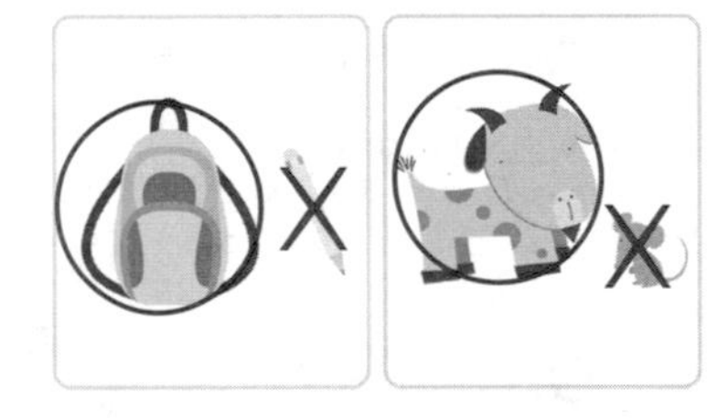

49

Page 50

Understanding Time

What time is it? Some things happen during the day and some things happen at night. Draw a line from the time of day to the matching picture.

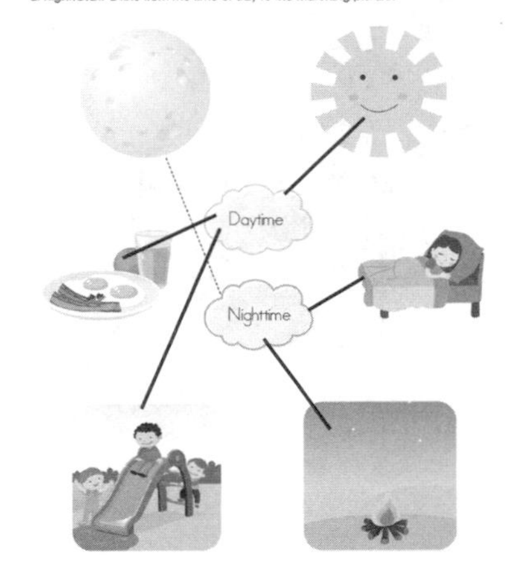

50

Page 51

Understanding Time

Let's Talk About a Clock!
A clock has numbers from 1 to 12 on its face. Complete the picture of the clock by writing the missing numbers in the circles.

51

Page 53

Sorting and Categorizing

Same
Circle the objects that are the same in each row.

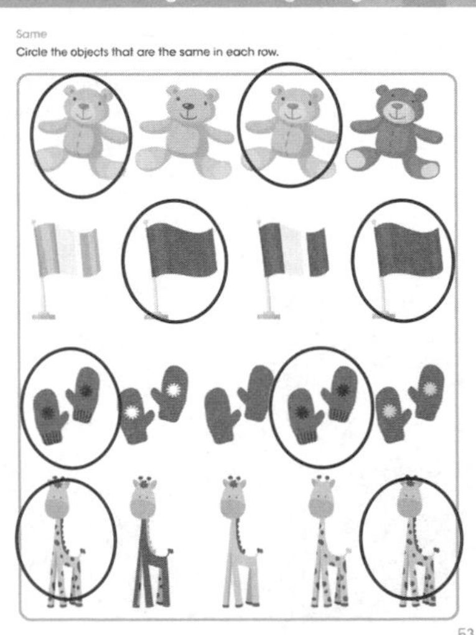

53

Page 54

Sorting and Categorizing

Different
Cross out the objects that are different in each row.

54

Page 55

Sorting and Categorizing

One of the things in each row doesn't belong there.
Cross out the objects that don't belong.

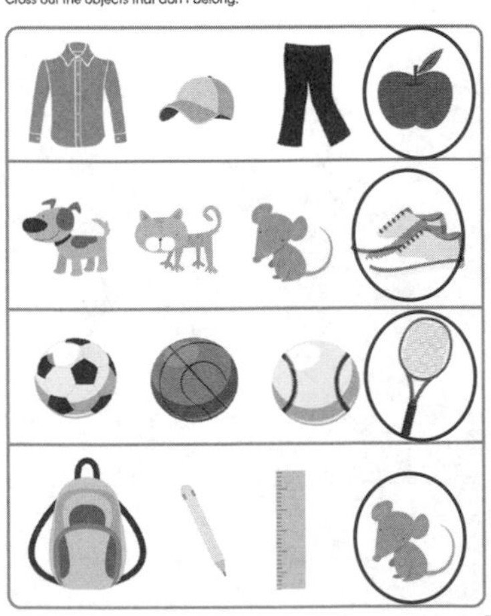

55

Page 56

Sorting and Categorizing

Graphing Shapes

Color in the graph to show how many of each shape is in the picture below.

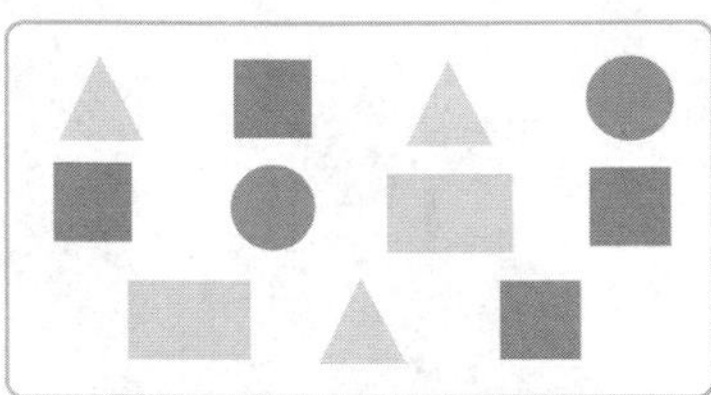

Shapes

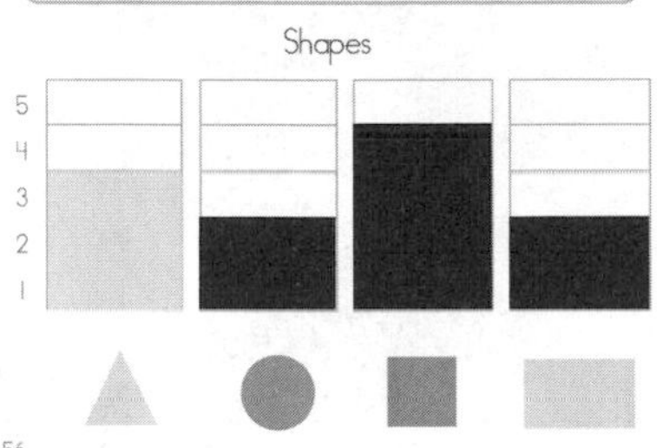

Page 57

Sorting and Categorizing

Reading a Bar Graph

Each colored section represents one person who likes that sport. Count how many votes each sport received and answer the questions below.

How many people like football? 6

How many people like soccer? 3

How many people like basketball? 5

How many people like baseball? 9

Our Favorite Sports

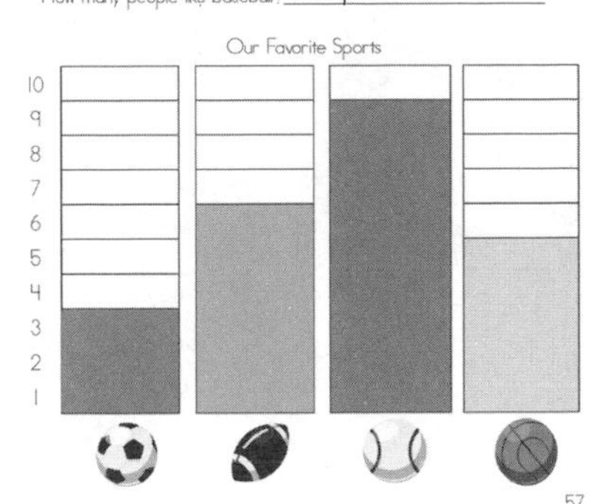

CERTIFICATE
of Achievement

....

has successfully completed

Kindergarten Math Workbook

Date: ....

Signed: ....